Punchneedle
Fun

Unique and Colorful Projects

Amy Bell Buehler

Martingale®
& COMPANY

Dedication

The creation of this book came as no surprise to my family. I am so grateful to have been blessed with loving parents, Lloyd and Anne Bell, who have highly praised and encouraged my creative endeavors since I was a little girl. According to them, there is nothing I can't do. Can you hear them cheering now? I am also thankful for a wonderful sister who has always made me feel special—thank you, Laura, for being my best friend, sounding board, and cattle prod. My everlasting love to Bill for not minding the mess in the sewing—I mean dining—room, and to our three wonderful children, Will, Steven, and Mae, for being so helpful and patient.

Punchneedle Fun: Unique and Colorful Projects
© 2007 by Amy Bell Buehler

That Patchwork Place® is an imprint of
Martingale & Company®.

Martingale & Company
20205 144th Ave. NE
Woodinville, WA 98072-8478
www.martingale-pub.com

Credits

President & CEO: Tom Wierzbicki
Publisher: Jane Hamada
Editorial Director: Mary V. Green
Managing Editor: Tina Cook
Acquisitions & Development Editor:
    Karen Costello Soltys
Technical Editor: Carol A. Thelen
Copy Editor: Melissa Bryan
Design Director: Stan Green
Assistant Design Director: Regina Girard
Illustrator: Laurel Strand
Cover & Text Designer: Stan Green
Photographer: Brent Kane

Printed in China
12 11 10 09 08 07   8 7 6 5 4 3 2 1

Library of Congress Cataloging-in-Publication Data
Library of Congress Control Number: 2007007506

ISBN: 978-1-56477-754-6

Mission Statement

Dedicated to providing quality products and service to inspire creativity.

Contents

Introduction
Or How I Started Punching

Through my many visits to Kindred Quilts, a quilt shop in Clinton, New Jersey, I became drawn to punchneedle embroidery. I loved seeing the adorable framed projects displayed throughout the shop. It wasn't long before I gave in and bought a punchneedle along with a pattern to get started. As I read through the instructions, my mind immediately jumped into "what if?" mode, and my cube pincushion was born. I still haven't made the pattern I bought, nor have I framed anything!

If you're new to punchneedle embroidery, you may be quite surprised to discover how easy it is. Even if you make every mistake possible (like I have), the mistakes either are not apparent to others or are easily fixed! Once you learn the basic technique of punching, it is simply a matter of coloring in a design—a lot like painting by number. There's no counting of stitches; the projects are easily portable; and your finished product can be framed, used as an appliqué, applied to a pin back, or manipulated into a three-dimensional object! Of course you don't have to tell other people how easy it is. Let them be amazed by your work and think that you have spent countless hours making something just for them.

Don't be surprised if you become more and more drawn into punchneedle. I find myself checking the ads in the Sunday paper for sales on embroidery floss, looking for design inspirations and color combinations while running errands, and punching away on more than one project at a time! The more entranced I have become with punchneedle embroidery, the more I have wanted to know about

it. Did you know there is a difference between miniature punchneedle and traditional punchneedle? Miniature punchneedle uses primarily embroidery floss, the loops are set to a fairly uniform size, and the finished product is usually somewhat small. Traditional punchneedle uses other types of thread in addition to floss, such as two-ply acrylic yarn, metallic threads, and even ribbon, and employs a host of interesting loop techniques to achieve incredible beauty and depth in the finished work.

While this book deals primarily with miniature punchneedle, I have occasionally used two-ply yarn in these projects instead of floss with wonderful results. I encourage you to explore these other options in punchneedle embroidery.

Supplies

The Good Stuff

You'll need several items for punchneedle embroidery, and you may already have a few of them in your sewing supplies. Some are readily available at your local quilt shop, craft store, or discount store. Others, such as punchneedles, threaders, and specialty yarns, can be purchased through mail order or Internet vendors if you can't find them locally (see the list of resources on page 48).

Punchneedles

Punchneedles are available in several brands and styles. Probably the most common punchneedle is the type with a plastic handle. It comes in two styles; both are equally comfortable and easy to use. The Cameo Ultra-Punch is noted for the ease with which you can set the loop size by simply clicking a spring-loaded mechanism to a numbered setting. It is also easy to change the needle size, which is another great feature of this model. Other brands of plastic-handled punchneedles such as Pretty Punch and Purr-fect Punch come with one permanently affixed needle per handle, and the loop length is adjusted with the turn of a dial or knob. What I like about the plastic-handled models is that they are lightweight and fit very comfortably in my hand, even after several hours of punching. I also like how easy it is to "close up" the needle tip when I am finished punching.

Metal-handled punchneedles, such as the Super Luxo and Igolochkoy brands, are generally short and thin, and they feel a bit heavier in the hand. Loop length is adjusted by cutting a piece of plastic tubing (provided with the needle) and sliding it down the needle to the base. You need to cut a piece of this tubing for each size of loop you want

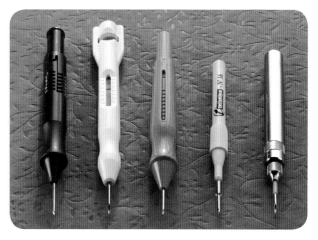

A variety of punchneedles, both plastic-handled and metal-handled models

to use. You may need to experiment with this; the loop length is about half the length from the eye of the needle to the base of the plastic.

Nearly all models of punchneedles come in three needle sizes: small, medium, and large. A few are also available in an extra-small size, which is suitable for very thin threads and is wonderful for the extremely fine, detailed work often seen in traditional punchneedle embroidery. The small needle is for fine detailed work using one or two strands of floss or thread. The medium needle is for three strands of floss or one strand of two-ply acrylic yarn or pearl cotton. The large needle is for using four to six strands of floss. Most punchneedles can be purchased as a set that includes all three basic sizes. If you wish to buy only one size to start with, I recommend the medium, which is the needle size I used for all the projects in this book.

It would be nice to live near a shop that offered every single make and model of punchneedle, so you could hold each one in your hand to decide which feels the most comfortable. Unfortunately, many shops carry only one or two brands. So think about the pens and pencils that you use every day. Is there one shape or length that you prefer over another? Do you find yourself looking for a particular kind of pen because you like the solid way it feels in your hand? Do you like to add a rubber grip to your pencils? The plastic-handled punchneedle may be the one for you if you prefer a full yet lightweight shape. The metal-handled types are great if you prefer a small but hefty feel. A rubber pencil grip is easy to add to some of these models. Although you might not find a large variety available locally, the Internet offers the full spectrum (see the list of resources on page 48).

Threader

After the punchneedle, the threader is the next most indispensable piece of equipment you will need, since you will not be able to thread your punchneedle without it. Most punchneedles include one or two of these in their packaging. Don't lose it! This hair-thin piece of folded wire with a white paper tag on the end seems to disappear on the floor if you drop it. I highly recommend that you do something to the paper tag to make it more visible. Color the paper with a fluorescent highlighter pen or tie a scrap of bright ribbon through it. Add anything you can think of to give it a bit of noticeable color to contrast against your floor and furniture. It is also a good idea to get into the habit of putting the threader back into your case after each use.

Floss and Yarn

Miniature punchneedle is noted for its use of six-strand cotton floss such as that from DMC and Anchor. This floss is available in a rainbow of colors and also comes in variegated and metallic

Paper tags and ribbon on the end of punchneedle threaders helps you find them if dropped. Not all threaders come with paper tags attached. These threaders are long enough that the paper and ribbon do not interfere with threading.

combinations. These are easy to find in your local craft and discount shops. Another option is the hand-dyed floss from Weeks Dye Works Inc. (see the list of resources on page 48). When possible, I have given the comparable color numbers for each of these brands in each project listing.

An alternative to floss is pearl cotton, which comes in several sizes and is also readily available in local craft and discount stores. Size 5 works quite well in the medium-size punchneedle. Pearl cotton creates a slightly larger and more defined loop than floss and adds a glossy sheen to the finished look. However, the color selection is not as wide as that of floss. This thread works nicely in most cases, but I find the loops are a little too thick to achieve fine points in my designs.

Traditional punchneedle typically uses a small two-ply acrylic yarn, which gives a wonderfully soft, plush feel to the design. These yarns fit a medium punchneedle and can also be combined with a single strand of metallic thread called angel hair to

Floss, pearl cotton, and two-ply acrylic yarn

Weavers cloth in natural and hand-dyed colors

add sparkle to the punched work. The yarns come in a number of colors, with 100 to 225 yards on a spool. There are several manufacturers of these yarns, including Pretty Punch, Purr-fect Punch, Dee Lite, and Cameo, and all the brands work extremely well together. These yarns are available through the Internet and mail order (see the list of resources on page 48).

Punching Fabric

Weavers cloth, a polyester and cotton blend, is the fabric of choice for punchneedle. The weave is tight enough to hold the loops, yet it forgives mistakes and allows you to repunch areas if necessary. Other fabrics can be suitable choices for punchneedle, but you should experiment with them first. Loosely woven fabrics, such as homespun, will not hold the loops. Likewise, fabrics with an extremely tight weave, such as batiks, are difficult to punch through without the sharp needle slicing the threads. There needs to be a little give to the threads to allow the sharp needle to separate them and glide through. Most weavers cloth is found in natural, white, and denim, and now Weeks Dye Works Inc. offers hand-dyed weavers cloth in 14 colors.

An assortment of snips and small scissors—the sharper, the better!

Scissors

A small pair of very sharp scissors or snips is a real necessity for cutting the threads close to your work. It is especially important that they be *sharp!* It's very discouraging to snip your final thread and accidentally pull out several loops instead. I love my Gingher embroidery scissors and thread snips, and I make a special point to keep them in my sewing or punchneedle case to avoid the temptation of using them to cut anything else nearby, such as newspaper coupons!

Hoops of various sizes

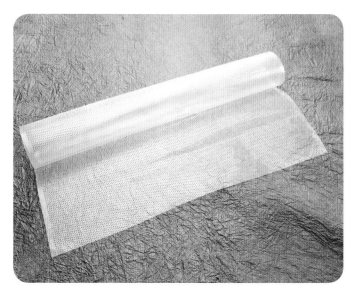

Mesh transfer material

Hoops

Forget about using your old wooden embroidery hoop, even if it is a spring-loaded one. The pressure of punching is much greater than that created by other forms of embroidery. The hoop must keep the fabric taut for effective punching. I think the Hoop-La lip-locking hoop from Susan Bates is wonderful. The interlocking lip edge does a terrific job of holding the fabric taut against the pressure applied with every punch of the needle. These colorful hoops are quite affordable and are found at craft and discount stores. They come in many round sizes, from 4" to 10", as well as two oval sizes. I find the most versatile size to be the 8" round hoop, but they are so inexpensive that I have one of every size! The projects in this book will indicate the smallest hoop size that can be used, but a larger one is fine provided your fabric is large enough to fit in it. My preference is to use a larger hoop so that I can punch more than one pattern or design without rehooping. For example, I will often fit a few bookmark squares around a larger pincushion pattern. Then I can punch all the designs before taking my work out of the hoop. If you put more than one design on your fabric, make sure to allow ¼" to ½" of space between each one.

Pattern-Transfer Materials and Methods

There are several methods of tracing patterns from the book to your fabric. Regardless of the method you choose, it is important to pay attention to the grain lines as you transfer the pattern. Although the interior of a design may have curved lines, usually the outside of a pattern is a square or rectangle. If at all possible, try to position the outside lines of the pattern so that they run along threads of your fabric. This will help to keep your lines straight while punching, and also when you stretch the fabric in the hoop.

My favorite transfer method is what I call a poor man's light box. Trace the pattern onto paper with a dark marker and tape the paper to a bright window. The light shining through the back of the paper makes it possible to see the outline through most fabrics. Now hold the fabric square up to the paper, center it over the pattern, and tape the fabric to the window so that it won't shift as you trace onto it. I do a lot of pattern tracing on a sunny day!

Another transfer method is the use of a plastic mesh such as that made by Clover. Place the mesh over the pattern and trace with a pencil. If you use an erasable pen or pencil, the mesh can be used over and over again. Next, center the mesh design on top of your fabric and retrace your previously marked lines. A pencil works well on most light to medium fabrics, and a chalk pencil shows up nicely on darker fabric. This will give something of a dot-to-dot effect on your fabric, but you can easily darken the lines by drawing over them with a marker.

I prefer using a fine-tip permanent marker on the fabric. I like to have a nice dark line with a sharp edge to follow when I am punching. If the marker tip is broad, the line comes out a bit fuzzy and it is difficult to keep a precise punching line.

Another important thing to remember when transferring a pattern onto your fabric is that it is the reverse of what the finished design will look like. For example, the Love That Cat pattern on page 24 is drawn with the cat facing right. But the completed design shows the cat facing left. Be aware of this when you plan your own designs. If you want to punch letters or numbers, you will need to trace them backward onto your fabric. The easiest way to do this is to create an image of the finished design on paper, turn it over, and retrace the design with a marker on the back of the paper. Then trace that side of the design onto your fabric.

Glue

For nearly all the projects in this book, the back of your punched design will need protection and strength for the further manipulation needed to complete construction. From the time I found fabric-glue products such as Fray Block, Liquid Stitch, and Aleene's line (shown above right), I

A variety of fabric glues for punchneedle projects

haven't looked back! A thin layer of any of these glues spread on the back of the loops keeps them from being pulled out accidentally, yet the fabric remains soft and pliable. The glue won't wash out. Spread it over the back of the work with your fingertip, let it dry, and then proceed with the project instructions. Please note that this is not your ordinary children's craft glue; this is fabric glue that is sold in most craft stores. This glue can be pretty sticky. A little vegetable oil helps wash the residue off your fingers.

Use a What?

For years one of my favorite and least expensive tools has been the lowly wooden cuticle stick. This little item, commonly sold in discount and drug stores, is very useful for both sewing and ironing. It also does a great job of poking out corners and stuffing all that fluffy fiberfill into tight spaces. I keep one by my sewing machine, one by the iron, and one in my portable sewing kit. If you have a fancier tool, by all means use it. But if you like to stretch your dollar, go get your cuticle sticks!

Preparation

This Won't Take Long

If you're an old hand at punchneedle, you probably already know what to do next. If you're new to punchneedle, don't be alarmed at all the steps involved in this form of embroidery. Once you get going, you will find that punchneedle really is quick and easy. Like all needlecrafts, reading the directions is the most time-consuming part! There are three things you need to do: position your design, centered and stretched, within the hoop; prepare your thread; and thread the needle.

Using the Hoop

When you separate the hoop into its inner and outer rings, you will notice that they look and feel different from your old wooden hoops. The outer ring is smooth and has a clamping screw to help it close tightly around the inner ring. The inner ring has a lipped ridge along one edge, which should always be on top.

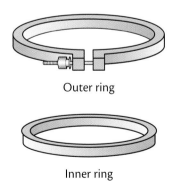

Outer ring

Inner ring

It helps to think of preparing the fabric in the hoop as making a sandwich: inner hoop, fabric, outer hoop. Place the inner ring on a flat surface with the lipped ridge on top. Lay the fabric on the ring, with the design facing up and centered in the circle. The outer hoop should be loosened nearly to the end of the screw to allow it to fit over the fabric and the lipped edge.

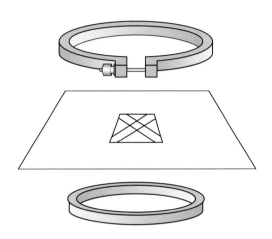

As you push the outer hoop down, you can almost feel it click over the lipped ridge and settle underneath. Alternately tighten the screw and gently tug on the fabric all the way around the hoop. The fabric must be drum-tight in the hoop for successful punching. Pay attention to the grain lines in the fabric as you pull the fabric ever tighter. You don't want to stretch the design out of shape by pulling one side more than another. It is helpful to practice this to get comfortable with it.

Preparing the Thread

Pearl cotton and two-ply acrylic yarn need no preparation other than cutting a long length to work with. The two-ply yarn is often used with a spool holder that attaches to the end of the handle, and you only cut the thread when you're finished punching a section.

Since most of these projects use embroidery floss, let's discuss that. Floss comes in 8.7-yard lengths, and you're getting twice that amount of thread because each length is further separated into two sections of three strands each. I prefer cutting off and using a very long length of thread, sometimes as long as 5 or 6 feet, depending on how much area I want to cover. Separating these long lengths of floss is often an exercise in frustration, since the thread wants to twist itself into a big snarl. My favorite method is to separate the first 6", stand up while holding one section of three strands in each hand, and then slowly pull them apart. By letting the floss hang unobstructed in the air, it is free to untwist. If I have cut a really long length, I will rotate my wrists so that the thread wraps around each hand. It is important to do this slowly so the separation isn't happening faster than the untwisting. Put one length of three-strand floss aside and thread the other into your punchneedle.

Threading the Punchneedle

No matter which punchneedle you choose, they are all threaded in the same way. As you look at the punchneedle, you will see that it consists of a long hollow shaft encased in a handle with a hole on the side near the sharp tip. Threading the needle is a two-part procedure. First, insert the threader into the shaft from the sharp tip all the way through the handle until the open end of the threader clears the handle.

The end of the threader will open slightly, and you will place the end of your floss through that opening, allowing a 2" to 3" tail.

Gently draw the threader back out of the needle and remove the floss from the threader. Now the

floss has been threaded through the hollow shaft.

The second part of threading involves getting the floss through the eye of the needle. Insert the threader through the eye of the needle as shown below; place the floss into the opened end of the threader and gently pull the threader back through the eye of the needle.

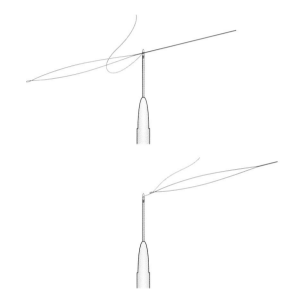

Remove the floss from the threader. At this point, the floss may extend 3" or more out from the needle tip. Gently draw all but about 1" back through the handle. Now you're ready to begin punching.

Remember to put your threader away in a safe place! I cannot emphasize this too strongly.

Once the needle is threaded, you will need to be careful as you work. It is extremely easy for that floss to slide right back out! You can pinch the thread against the needle for a moment to keep it from sliding out, but for those times when you must put the threaded punchneedle down quickly to answer the phone or the door, a great option is to slip a knitting-needle protector over the needle tip.

Let's Get Punching

Now that you've prepared your fabric in the hoop and threaded your needle, you're ready to begin. It is important to hold both the hoop and the needle comfortably in your hands and to always be aware of where your hoop hand and fingers are in relation to where the needle is punching.

It is helpful to have a plan for punching a design. For a pattern with many small areas of detail, such as the Love That Cat pattern on page 24, it is a good idea to work from the interior of the design outward. The smaller details such as the nose, whiskers, and eyes should be done first, and then the rest of the face should be filled in. This goes against the usual recommendation of punching all the areas of one color at a time. Patterns with less detail, such as quilt blocks, should be worked one color at a time. Begin by outlining the shape, and then fill it in. As you finish with one color and are ready to punch a new one next to the completed area, angle your needle slightly away from the previous loops to avoid punching into them. Note that punching is done from the wrong side. To see the loops, you'll need to turn the work over.

How to Punch

If you're right-handed, hold the hoop in your left hand and the needle in your right. Don't hold the hoop on a table, as you'll risk damaging the needle point on the hard surface. Don't hold the hoop in your lap, either, as you might punch a hole in yourself! Just hold it a little bit up in the air. You will find your comfortable position soon enough. I tend to hold the hoop so that one edge is slightly braced on a sofa arm or on my abdomen.

The punchneedle should be held upright over the fabric. While I hold my punchneedle the same way I hold a pencil, I still keep it pretty much at a 90° angle to the fabric. This keeps my loops from forming at too much of an angle. Only when you're punching one color next to another should you angle your needle a bit so that the new loops don't tangle with the previous ones.

Notice the beveled edge of the needle. It should always be facing the direction of travel. If the beveled edge faces the wrong direction, your loops will be pulled out because you'll be punching through the thread as well as the fabric!

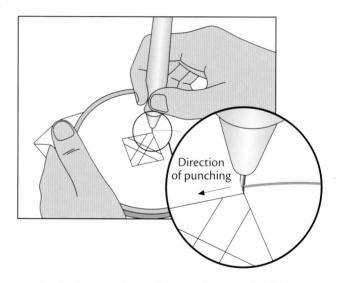

Direction of punching

Push the punchneedle straight into the fabric, all the way down until it won't go any farther. Depending on your needle, either the plastic gauge or the handle itself will be the stopping point. It is important that you always push the needle down this far, as this is what makes uniform loops.

Pull the needle back up gently and slide it over about a needle's width to make the next stitch. It will feel a little bit like you're scraping the needle along the fabric. Do not raise the needle above the fabric or you will pull out all or part of your previous loop. There should be about a needle's width between each loop as well as between each row of loops, but who wants to do that much measuring? Just think of it as moving over a few threads for each loop. You will quickly get a feel for the spacing as your rhythm picks up.

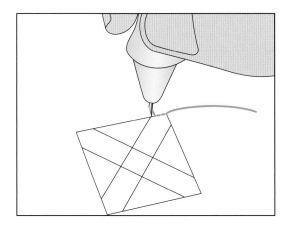

If you're right-handed, you will be punching from right to left; if left-handed, you will punch from left to right. Try to punch your design in a uniform manner, whether it is in straight lines or curves. Keep the loops evenly spaced as you fill in an area. Straight lines are easier if you can follow a thread in the fabric. As you reach the end of a row of loops and need to change direction, gently keep the needle tip in the fabric and turn the hoop, not the needle. This will keep the beveled edge facing the new direction of travel.

If you turn the work over at this point, you may be disappointed. The loops seem to be shapeless and messy looking. Relax. Once an area is filled, and another, and another, a beautiful design takes shape. It takes many loops punched together to make the whole picture.

After you finish a section or need to stop to change colors, use your fingernail or a scissor tip to hold the thread down firmly as you lift the needle up and away. Snip the thread close to the fabric.

You also need to snip your beginning thread close to the fabric to avoid accidentally snagging it and pulling out loops.

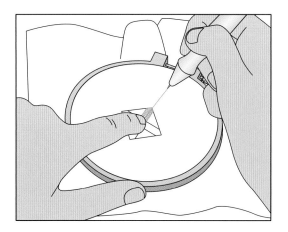

Checking Your Work

Flip your work over before finishing with a color to check for bare spots. If an area looks a little sparse, go back and punch a few more loops to fill in the space. You might as well do it now while you still have the same color thread in your needle. If you're not happy with the loops or with the color you used, you can pull the loops out. Use your fingernail to scrape across the empty holes before punching new loops. The beauty of weavers cloth is that it allows you to remove thread and repunch without damaging the fabric.

Punching into another loop will happen no matter how much you try to avoid it, but it won't ruin your work! If you have punched into a loop of a different color, you can use a stiletto, pin, or needle to gently pry the one loop out of the other. This sounds difficult, but it takes only a second to do. Another problem you may notice is a loop that sticks out farther than the others. Simply use your sharp scissors and trim it. I caution you to try not to be too much of a perfectionist—before you know it, there may not be a single loop left to trim! Those little waves of loops add to the overall look and texture that make punchneedle unique.

The more you use your punchneedle, the more comfortable you will become with it. Start off with small projects such as the bookmarks on page 16 that are only 1" in size. Give yourself the freedom to experiment with different colors and threads as well as various loop depths. While you may see some uneven loops or wobbling lines, others will see only perfection in the final product!

Almost Finished

As you punch, try to be aware of the thread coming out the back of the punchneedle handle. If it gets pinned under your arm (or a furry companion curls up on top of it), you will feel a stretching of the thread and then no longer be able to make loops. I suggest laying that thread across the top of your punching hand where you can see it. Since the thread usually begins as a very long length, you should also watch for any tangles. It can be difficult to remove a snarl once it gets inside the handle.

After you have punched the entire design and have turned it over to check for any problems, remove it from the hoop. You will need three things to prepare the back of the work: an iron, fabric glue, and scissors. Don't forget the handy cuticle stick, as well. I use it as an extra finger when holding down a folded section to be pressed. It hurts a lot less to burn the cuticle stick than my fingers!

Place a fluffy towel on your ironing board. I like to use a towel when pressing so that the loops don't lose their fluffiness. Lay the fabric, loop side down, on top of the towel. If you have punched very tightly, your work may be curled up somewhat. Take note of this and try not to punch as heavily in your next project. The curling can be remedied with careful pressing.

With a warm iron, gently press the punched design. If you like, you can use steam to do this as well. A press cloth is not necessary for this part, but I like to use one. My iron and I have a love-hate relationship. I love what it can do, but I hate what happens when I get distracted! Turn your work over and quickly slide the iron right next to the loops on all sides. This helps the loops on the edge stand up straight so that when you cut the excess fabric away later, you won't accidentally cut loops as well.

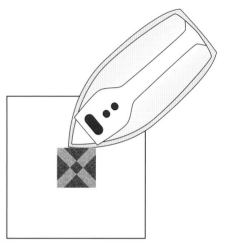

Turn the work back over. Using a fingertip, apply a light layer of fabric glue to the back of the loops. I also cover about ¼" of the fabric along the outside edge of the loops. Wipe off any excess.

The fabric glue keeps the fabric from unraveling even if it is cut a thread's width away from the loops. It also locks each loop in place so well that the finished piece can be washed and dried. Let the glue dry for the recommended length of time before proceeding. At this point, you will need to refer to each project's finishing instructions.

The Projects
Make Them All

If you're like me, you looked at the pictures and went straight to the first project that you want to make. Remember, there is a lot of information in the preceding sections if you need it!

Each project includes a thread chart listing the colors used in each specific pattern, but please feel free to change the colors to suit your own preference. Experiment with color combinations and if you aren't happy, pull out the loops and start over. The thread charts give the color number or both color number and name, according to each manufacturer; the two-ply yarn is listed by color name only.

Every project was completed using a medium punchneedle. The loop depth is set low, meaning the loops are short. This is either a 1 or 2 setting on the Cameo Ultra-Punch and Purr-fect Punch, and an A or B setting on the Pretty Punch. If using a metal-handled punchneedle, you will need to cut a piece of plastic gauge approximately ¼" long to achieve the same depth to the loops. If you prefer longer loops in any project, be aware the finished project will not look exactly the same as pictured here.

Many variations are possible for several of these designs. For example, the cube pincushion would make a wonderful Christmas ornament worked in holiday-themed colors; sew a folded ribbon into a seam to create a hanging loop. In any pattern based on a square shape, almost any quilt block can be substituted. You can experiment by drawing only the outside lines of the pattern and then filling in the space with your own design. Feel free to change any or all of the colors, fabrics, buttons, and ribbons, and make the finished product truly yours.

Bookmarks

Bet You Can't Make Just One

An assortment of pretty bookmarks • Finished size of punching: 1" x 1"

This is a great project for beginners and experts alike. You can tuck one into a gift book or in a card with a gift certificate to a bookstore. Use one to attach gift cards to packages. These make up so quickly that you will soon have one for every person on your list, if not for every book in your house! Although you can choose to leave the end of the bookmark's ribbon hanging freely, consider adding a special touch by making a duplicate square to put at the end of the ribbon or knotting a pretty bead onto the ribbon as pictured. Almost any ribbon will work well for this; I have used grosgrain, wired, satin, silk, and velvet. The only requirement for the ribbon is that it should be narrow—$^1/_4$" or less.

Materials

- 5" embroidery hoop
- 7" square of weavers cloth or other fabric
- Marking pen or pencil
- Punchneedle with medium (3-strand) needle
- Fabric glue
- Felt scraps, 1½" square (1 for each bookmark in a coordinating color)
- 15" to 18" length of narrow (¼" wide or less) ribbon (1 for each bookmark in a coordinating color)
- Bead, ¼" to ½" diameter (optional)

EMBROIDERY FLOSS (3 Strands) or YARN (1 Strand)

This chart lists floss and yarn selections from various suppliers. For each bookmark, choose one supplier. The box where the supplier column and bookmark row intersect shows the colors you'll need. Bookmark patterns are shown on page 19.

Bookmark	DMC	Anchor	Weeks	2-ply Yarn
Maple Leaf	801, 3052, 3853	358, 860, 330	2237-Hazelnut, 2200-Kudzu, 2228-Pumpkin	Brown, green, orange
Rail Fence	321, 803, Blanc	46, 134, 1	2269-Liberty, 1307-Americana, 1091-Whitewash	Red, blue, white
Pinwheel		1335, 1	4123-Celebration, 1091-Whitewash	
Italian Block	722, 309	316, 68	2226-Carrot, 2274-Romance	Orange, rose
Streak of Lightning	801, 776	358, 25	2237-Hazelnut, 2229-Sweetheart Rose	Brown, pink
Quarter-Square Triangles	3752, Blanc	144, 1	2109-Morris Blue, 1091-Whitewash	Blue, white
Shooting Star			2217-Lemon Chiffon, 3910-Mascara	Yellow, black
Dots	3752, 801	144, 358	2109-Morris Blue, 2237-Hazelnut	Blue, brown
Tree Everlasting	3362, Ecru	218, 885	1277-Collards, 3500-Sand	Green, cream
Bowtie	310, 519	403, 928	3900-Kohl, 2131-Aqua	Black, aqua

Punching the Design

1. Mark as many as four patterns in the center of the weavers cloth, leaving ¼" to ½" of space between each pattern. You'll want the patterns about ½" from the edge of the hoop. A good way to keep in mind the outline of the hoop is to lightly trace the inside of the hoop circle on your fabric. Then as you trace your patterns within that space, you will stay at least ½" from that edge.

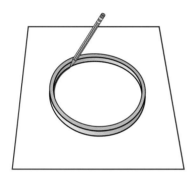

2. Center the design in the hoop, referring to "Using the Hoop" on page 10.
3. Using three strands of floss, start with one color and fill each section for that color. Remember to snip the beginning and ending threads of each section close to the work.
4. After each design is completely punched, follow the instructions in "Almost Finished" on page 14.
5. Using sharp scissors and working from the front of your piece, carefully cut out each square just along the edge of the loops, leaving only the width of a thread or two of fabric.

Constructing the Bookmark

1. For each bookmark, cut a felt square slightly larger than the punched squares. Cut a 15" to 18" length of coordinating ribbon for each. Decide on the ribbon placement—do you want it to extend from the center of the square or from the corner?
2. Apply a light layer of glue to one side of the felt and lay one end of the ribbon on top of it. Put a drop of glue on the top of the ribbon.

3. Place the punched square on top of the felt and ribbon, sliding it as needed to center it on the felt. When you're satisfied with the placement, press together firmly and set aside to dry.
4. When the bookmark is dry, trim the excess felt from the edge. May you never lose your place again!

Construction Options

Experiment with the following fun bookmark variations.

- Attach a second square to the opposite end of the ribbon, following the same steps above.

- String a bead on the free end of the ribbon and tie a knot at the end of the ribbon to secure the bead.
- Use two ribbons in coordinating or contrasting colors. In step 2 of "Constructing the Bookmark," decide which ribbon you want on top and place the ribbons accordingly. Put a drop of glue between each ribbon.

Maple Leaf   Rail Fence   Pinwheel   Italian Block   Streak of Lightning

Quarter-Square Triangles   Shooting Star   Dots   Tree Everlasting   Bowtie

Bookmark patterns and color keys

Needle Book

Now I Know Where It Is

Two lovely needle books for your projects • Finished size of punching: approximately 2" x 2½"

I love to do hand appliqué but never seem to be able to find my favorite straw needles in their little plastic case. These needle books are perfect for making sure you always have needles handy. The felt for the book is cut large, giving you plenty of room to trim it down as much or as little as desired after your punchneedle design is added. Quick and easy to make, you may find yourself tucking one of these into each of your sewing projects.

Your needles safely stored inside!

Materials

- For each needle book:
  - 7" square of weavers cloth or other fabric
  - 3½" x 7" piece of felt for cover
  - 2½" x 6" piece of contrasting felt for pages

- 5" embroidery hoop

- Marking pen or pencil

- Punchneedle with medium (3-strand) needle

- Fabric glue

- Cuticle stick or Hera marker from Clover

- Sewing machine or sewing needle and coordinating thread

- 2 ribbons or yarn scraps in 15" lengths and tapestry needle (optional)

- Pinking shears (optional)

EMBROIDERY FLOSS (3 Strands) or YARN (1 Strand)				
This chart lists floss and yarn selections from various suppliers. For each needle book, choose one supplier. The box where the supplier column and needle book row intersect shows the colors you'll need.				
Needle Book	**DMC**	**Anchor**	**Weeks**	**2-ply Yarn**
Amish Mosaic		403, 98, 433, 33, 203		Black, purple, teal, red, green
Flower Pot	3908, Ecru, 3712, 3052, 729, 801	168, 926, 1024, 859, 307, 358	1282-Ocean, 6650-Buttercup, 2245-Grapefruit, 2200-Kudzu, 2219-Whiskey, 2237-Hazelnut	

Punching the Design

1. Trace the pattern onto the center of the weavers cloth, and then hoop the fabric with the design centered. See "Using the Hoop" on page 10.
2. Starting with one color and using three strands of floss or the two-ply yarn, outline and fill each section for that color. Continue in this manner until all colors are used.
3. After the design is completely punched, follow the instructions in "Almost Finished" on page 14.

Constructing the Needle Book

1. Center the smaller piece of felt on top of the larger one. Draw a line down the center of the layered pieces with the point of a cuticle stick or the edge of a Hera marker. This will leave a depression in the felt that is easy to see.

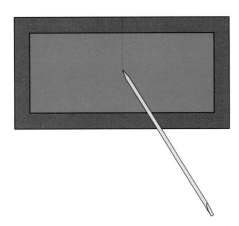

2. Fold the felt in half along the depression line. Use either of these methods to sew the book:
   - Use your sewing machine to sew through all four layers a scant ¼" from the fold line.
   - Thread a tapestry needle with the ribbon or yarn and sew large Xs over the fold. Start sewing at the bottom, leaving about 3" of the ribbon or yarn hanging. The ribbon stitches should be ½" or slightly farther apart and ⅜" from the folded edge. Sew up to the top, leaving about 3" hanging. Cut the ribbon or yarn.

   Thread the tapestry needle with a different ribbon or yarn and sew large Xs over the fold. Start sewing at the top, leaving about 3" of the ribbon or yarn hanging, and sew to the bottom, leaving about 3" hanging. Cut the ribbon or yarn. Tie the two ends into small bows and secure with a drop of glue.

3. With loops facing toward you, cut out the punched design along the edge of the loops. After cutting on all four sides, turn over and trim any excess. Only a thread or two should be visible along the edge.
4. Spread a light layer of glue on the back of the punched design. The previous layer of glue locked in the loops; this layer will glue it to the felt. By sight, center the design on the top of the needle book. Once you're satisfied with its placement, press firmly and allow it to dry. Trim the felt as much or as little as you like. Use pinking shears for a different look.

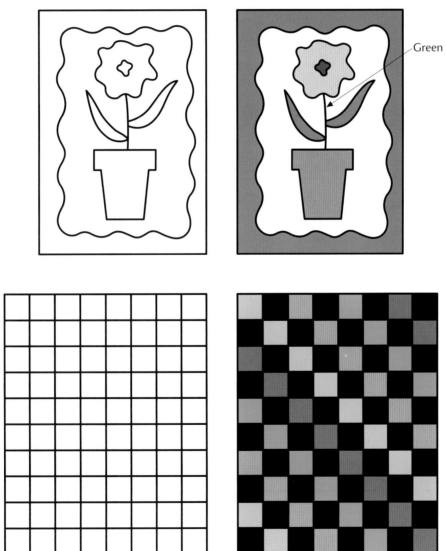

Green

**Needle book patterns
and color keys**

Punchneedle Case

Love That Cat

Punchneedle cases in two styles
Finished size of punching: approximately 2½" x 3½" • Finished size: 5" x 8¾", closed

Everything in its place and a place for everything: a case for the punchneedle and threader is almost a necessity! After finding the threader on the floor and losing the punchneedle among my pens and pencils, I decided to make a case to keep them together. Although the directions seem long, this case goes together quickly. I love finding a special button to match my fabric, but if you don't want to bother making a buttonhole, sew on a hook-and-loop closure instead. The two pockets inside hold all the essentials. The smaller one is perfect for 4" scissors, and the other, formed by folding up the bottom of the rectangle, is deep enough to hold the punchneedle and threader.

Any punchneedle design will dress up and personalize your punchneedle case. The whimsical cat pattern I used for this project was drawn by my young daughter a few years ago. It looks great either as a black-and-white line drawing or in bright colors to match your fabric.

Materials

- 5½" x 23" piece each of outer fabric, batting, and inner fabric
- 5½" x 8" piece of contrasting fabric for inner pocket
- Button
- Sewing machine
- Sewing needle and thread
- Cuticle stick
- ½" square of hook-and-loop tape (optional)
- 6" embroidery hoop
- 8" square of weavers cloth or other fabric
- Marking pen or pencil
- Punchneedle with medium (3-strand) needle
- Fabric glue

EMBROIDERY FLOSS (3 Strands) or YARN (1 Strand)				
This chart lists floss and yarn selections from various suppliers. For each punchneedle case, choose one supplier. The box where the supplier column and punchneedle case row intersect shows the colors you'll need.				
Punchneedle Case	**DMC**	**Anchor**	**Weeks**	**2-ply Yarn**
Cat with Color		1090, 158, 403, 187, 1092	2118-Blue Topaz, 2109-Morris Blue, 3900-Kohl, 2141-Lagoon, 2129-Robin's Egg	Teal, light blue, black, green, light green
Black-and-White Cat	310, Blanc	403, 1	3900-Kohl, 1091-Whitewash	Black, white

Constructing the Case

1. Layer the inner and outer fabrics with right sides together. With the outer fabric on the bottom, place the layers on top of the batting. Sew ¼" all the way around, leaving a 3" section open along one side as shown.

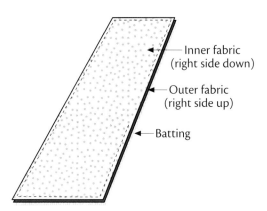

Inner fabric
(right side down)

Outer fabric
(right side up)

Batting

2. Turn the fabrics right side out so that the batting is now in the middle. Use your cuticle stick to help push out the corners. Fold in the edges of the opening ¼". Using sewing needle and thread, stitch the opening closed. Press to give the edges a sharp crease.

3. Machine or hand quilt the three layers together as desired. Simple lines or meandering curves work quite well.

4. To make the inner pocket, fold each long edge of the pocket fabric in ¼" and press. Then fold the fabric in half so that it measures 5" x 4". Press to make a sharp fold line.

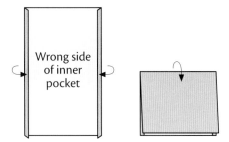

Wrong side
of inner
pocket

5. Place the quilted rectangle, inner fabric up, on your work surface, and then place the fold of the inner pocket 12" up from one short edge. Sew the inner pocket to the rectangle with a ½" seam allowance across the bottom raw edges of the pocket.

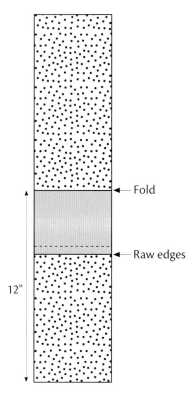

Fold

Raw edges

12"

6. Fold up the bottom of the case so that it measures 5½" from the fold to the top edge. The top edge will be 1" below the fold of the inner pocket. Center your button about 1" to 1½"

from the bottom fold and mark its placement. Open the case and hand sew the button in place.

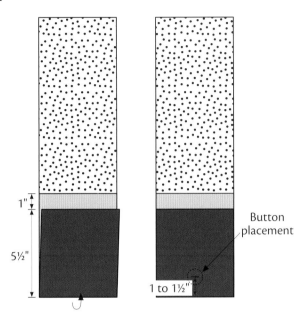

7. Fold the bottom edge of the case back up and sew close to the edge of each side, beginning at the top of the inner pocket and down 6½" to the case fold line. Your case is nearly complete!

8. Now fold down the top edge of the case and mark the placement and width of the buttonhole. Open the top edge and sew a buttonhole on your marked line. Once your buttonhole is stitched, slit it open with a seam ripper. Button your case closed. *Note:* If you don't have a fancy sewing machine to do buttonholes for you, just forget it and sew on hook-and-loop tape!

Punching the Design

1. Trace the pattern onto the center of the weavers cloth, and then hoop the fabric with the design centered. See "Using the Hoop" on page 10.

2. Start punching inner details including the eyes, nose, mouth, and whiskers first, and work your way outward, even though this will mean extra thread changes.

3. After the design is completely punched, follow the instructions in "Almost Finished" on page 14.

4. Working from the front of the design, carefully cut just outside the loops. Turn the punched piece over and trim more from the edge if necessary. Apply a second light layer of fabric glue. This application of glue will secure the design to the case.

5. With the case buttoned up, center the cat design to your liking. When you're satisfied with its placement, press firmly and allow it to dry.

Punchneedle case pattern

Fat-Quarter Punchneedle Case

Very Polished Looking

Punchneedle cases from fat quarters • Finished size: 5" x 8½", closed

Here is a project for some fun fat quarters. Minor changes were made to the size and construction of the previous punchneedle case to accommodate the use of a fat quarter of fabric. Other design changes include the binding and magnetic closure. Enjoy using novelty fabrics for this project. This case has two pockets: a small one for your 4" scissors and a larger one to hold your punchneedle and threader.

Finding fabric with a motif of sewing items inspired me to do something with a few of the old empty wooden spools gathering dust in my sewing room. With punched "thread" and pretty ribbons, these add an adorable little touch. Punch your spools in colors that coordinate with your fabric. If you don't have any wooden spools, empty plastic spools work just as well. Each pattern is made individually to fit each spool. I hope you enjoy making these as much as I have.

Materials

For the case:

- 5" x 17½" piece each of outer fabric, batting, and inner fabric

- 5" x 8" piece of fabric for small pocket

- 5" x 12" piece of fabric for large pocket

- 5" x 6" piece of batting

- 2 pieces of stiff interfacing (each about 2" square)

- ¾"-diameter magnetic closure

- 2½" x 52" strip of fabric for binding

- Seam ripper

- Medium or large safety pin

For the punchneedle design:

- 5" embroidery hoop

- 7" square of weavers cloth or other fabric

- Marking pen or pencil

- Embroidery floss or yarn

- Punchneedle with medium (3-strand) needle

- Fabric glue

- 2 wooden spools

- Scrap paper for measuring spool diameter

- 22" length of coordinating ribbon, ⅛" to ¼" wide

Constructing the Needle Case

The needle case is assembled and quilted, and then the two inner pockets are prepared and attached to the case with binding.

Assembling and Quilting the Case

1. Layer the inner fabric right side up on top of the batting.

2. The magnetic closure comes in four pieces: a thick half that locks to a thinner half, and a washer for each. The top and bottom halves each have two prongs that must be inserted through the fabric, and then the washer slides on and the two prongs are bent out to lock them into place. Center the larger half of the magnetic closure 1½" from the left edge as shown. Use a pencil to lightly mark where the two prongs of the magnetic closure touch the fabric.

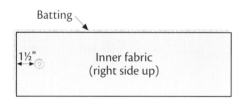

3. Use your seam ripper to make a small slit at each mark through both the fabric and the batting. Remove the washer from the magnetic closure. From the fabric side, insert the two prongs through the slits. You may need to push the batting down over the prongs. Place the washer back on the prongs as shown and push them out to lock the magnetic half in place.

4. Place the inner fabric and batting right side down and layer the outer fabric right side up on top as shown. Lift up the outer fabric and place a piece of stiff interfacing between the prongs and the outer fabric for support. A drop of glue to keep the interfacing in place is a good idea.

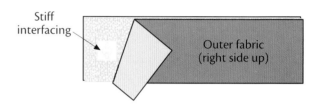

5. Machine quilt as desired. Straight lines or large circles work well. To avoid hitting the prongs, do not quilt within at least ¼" of the magnetic closure.

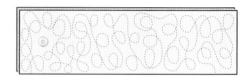

Preparing the Pockets

1. For the small pocket, fold the 5" x 8" piece of fabric in half, wrong sides together, so that it measures 5" x 4". Press. Lay the quilted needle case on your work surface and position the folded edge of the pocket 7" from the right edge of the case (the end without the magnetic closure). Using a ½" seam allowance, sew along the bottom raw edge to secure the pocket to the case.

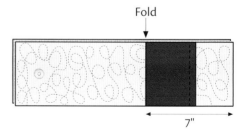

2. For the large pocket, place the 5" x 6" piece of batting on your work surface and layer the 5" x 12" piece of fabric, right side up, on top.

Measure 1½" from the edge as shown and place the thin half of the magnetic closure on top. When completed, this edge will be the bottom of the pocket and needle case.

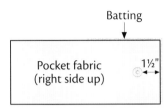

Batting

Pocket fabric (right side up)   1½"

3. Lightly mark where the two prongs touch the fabric. Use your seam ripper to make a small slit at both marks through the fabric and the batting, and install the magnetic closure as you did for the needle case.

4. Fold the excess fabric over the batting to make another quilt sandwich. Adding a drop of glue to keep it in place, insert the other piece of stiff interfacing between the prongs and fabric, and machine quilt as done previously, being careful not to sew too close to the magnetic closure.

5. Place the needle case on your work surface with the small pocket facing up. Place the large pocket on top, magnetic closure facing out, and line up the right edges as shown. Pin in place. Trim the raw edges before applying the binding.

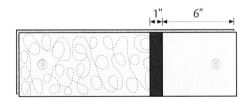

1"   6"

Binding the Edges

1. To prepare the binding strip, cut one end at a 45° angle and turn under ¼". Then fold in half lengthwise, wrong sides together, and press.

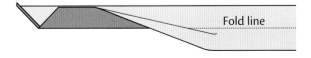

Fold line

2. The binding is stitched to the *outside* of the needle case. Leaving a 4" tail, lay the binding strip along one side of the rectangle, raw edges together. Begin sewing in the center of a long edge with a ¼" seam allowance, and stitch until your needle is ¼" from the corner.

3. Stop stitching, leaving your needle down. Raise your presser foot and rotate the needle case 45° clockwise so that the corner is pointing toward you. Lower your presser foot and stitch toward the corner, stitching off the edge.

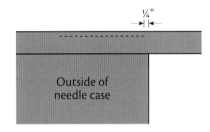

¼"

Outside of needle case

4. Fold the binding over the stitched angle, then fold it back onto itself so the raw edges of the binding and the needle case are even along the next edge. Begin stitching at the corner and continue stitching until the needle is ¼" from the next corner.

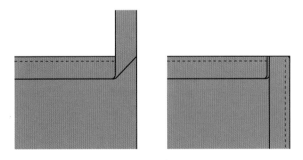

5. Repeat steps 3 and 4 until all four corners are complete. After the last corner, continue to stitch the binding to about 4" from the beginning.

6. When you reach the beginning of the binding, cut the end 1" longer than needed and tuck the end inside the beginning. Stitch the rest of the binding.

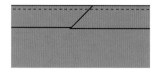

7. Bring the folded edge of the binding over the raw edges and hand sew to the inside of the case. As you reach each corner, fold one side down and then the other to make mitered corners. Use a pin to hold the edges in place if necessary as you sew.

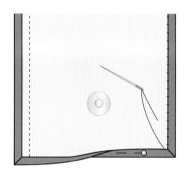

Punching the Design

1. Because wooden spools have varying diameters, no pattern is given. To make your pattern, cut a strip of paper the width of the body of the spool. Wrap the paper around the body and mark where it overlaps.

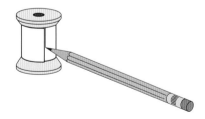

2. Cut on the marked line and discard the excess paper. Wrap the paper around the base again to check the measurement, and then lay the paper near the center of your weavers cloth and trace around it. Make a separate pattern for each spool you plan to cover. Generally, two spools will fit in a 5" hoop.

3. Hoop the fabric with the design in the center. See "Using the Hoop" on page 10.

4. Starting at one end, punch in lines as straight as possible. Use one color for each spool. Punch slightly outside the lines of the short sides of your rectangles.

5. After the design is completely punched, follow the instructions in "Almost Finished" on page 14.

6. Working from the front, carefully cut out the design right along the edge of the loops on the two long sides and one short side. Leave ⅛" on the other short side. Spread a light layer of glue on the back of the design and on top of the ⅛" edge.

7. Place the ribbon as shown, with about 10" extending out one side and 12" on the other. Wrap the punched design around the spool. Bring the two edges together and press firmly on all sides of the spool. Set aside to dry and repeat for the next spool.

8. When the spools are dry, lace the longer end of the ribbon through the center of the spool. Hold both ends and loop into a knot about 1" from the spool. Repeat for the other spool.

9. Tie the ribbon ends into a bow. Position the bow as desired on the case. Use a safety pin to secure the bow and attach it to the case from the inside. This large safety pin can do double duty by holding skeins of floss inside the case.

Cube Pincushion

It's Easier than It Looks

Four 1½" cube pincushions in quilt block designs. For ornaments, use holiday colors and designs and sew a folded length of ribbon into one of the seams.
Finished size of punching: approximately 1½" x 1½" each side of cube

Doesn't the sight of pincushions inspire you to be creative? These cube pincushions can echo your love of color and quilting. The patterns are based on 1¹/₂" squares. You can punch five sides in the same color or use a different color for each side. Another design decision to consider is whether you want to punch both the top and the bottom of the pincushion. Four patterns are provided, but the construction method will be the same no matter which design you choose. Because a square of template plastic is added to the bottom of the cube for stability, you must determine which is the top and which is the bottom before you begin the construction process. I do recommend that the top be a different color or pattern than the bottom so you don't get frustrated trying to stick pins in the side with the plastic!

Although I prefer to punch the top piece separately, the cube can also be punched as a complete six-sided design. Simply add a sixth square to the pattern above the C square. Construction will remain the same with one less side to join.

Materials

- 8" embroidery hoop
- 10" square of weavers cloth or other fabric for each pincushion
- 2" square of coordinating weavers cloth for top (optional)
- Marking pen or pencil
- Punchneedle with medium (3-strand) needle
- Fabric glue
- Cuticle stick
- 1⅜" square of template plastic for each pincushion
- Sewing needle and thread
- Fiberfill

EMBROIDERY FLOSS (3 Strands) or YARN (1 Strand)

This chart lists floss and yarn selections from various suppliers. For each pincushion, choose one supplier. The box where the supplier column and pincushion row intersect shows the colors you'll need.

Pincushion	DMC	Anchor	Weeks	2-ply Yarn
Nine-Patch	Ecru, 3712, 3052, 3768, 160	387, 1024, 859, 921, 121	1109-Angel Hair, 258-Aztec Red, 2200-Kudzu, 2104-Deep Sea, 2337-Periwinkle	
Triangles in a Square		387, 313, 260, 928, 870		
Orange Peel	777, Ecru	44, 387	1339-Bordeaux, 1109-Angel Hair	Brick, natural
Log Cabin	**Darks:** 3810, 3834, 367, 930, 3830, 777 **Lights:** 945, 3855, 3047, 3023, 778, Ecru			**Darks:** teal, purple, green, blue, orange, brick **Lights:** peach, yellow, lemon, sage, pink, natural

Punching the Design

1. Trace the pattern onto the center of the weavers cloth. To prevent having stretchy bias edges on your sewing lines, try to place the pattern lines so that they follow threads in your fabric. If you are going to punch the top as a separate piece, trace that onto your fabric as well. Place the fabric in the hoop with the design centered. See "Using the Hoop" on page 10.

2. Starting with any color you wish, punch an outline row and then fill in each section for that color. Even if a color flows from one square block to another, try to keep each square's pattern separate from another by punching an outline row first.

3. After the design is completely punched, follow the instructions in "Almost Finished" on page 14.

4. Cut out the punched work, leaving a generous ¼" seam allowance around all edges. Clip the inner angles as shown. Carefully fold each side to the back along the edge of the loops and press. Use the cuticle stick to hold the edge down as you press. Pressing gives a sharp crease, which makes a nice sewing line to follow.

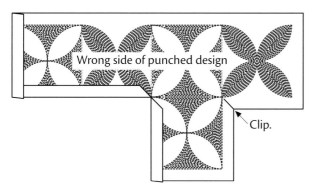

Wrong side of punched design

Clip.

Constructing the Pincushion

Note that each square in the diagram below is labeled with a letter, and each open edge is labeled with a number.

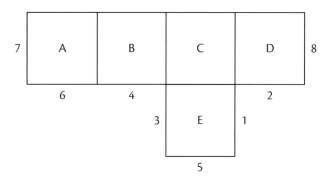

1. Referring to the diagram, bring edges 1 and 2 together with the loops on the outside. Pinch the edges together and sew by hand with a whipstitch from end to end. Since the pincushion will be stuffed with fiberfill, it is very important that you keep the stitches small and as close as possible to the edge of the loops. Use your needle to gently sweep stray loops out of the way as you sew. Knot the thread and leave the thread tail inside the cube.

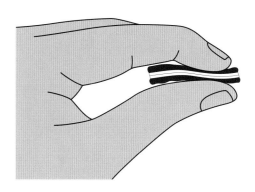

2. Bring edges 3 and 4 together and whipstitch them closed. Take a few extra stitches at the end for security. Bring edges 5 and 6 together and whipstitch them closed. Knot the thread and leave the tail hanging inside the cube.

3. At this point, the bottom of the cube is joined on all sides. Now you're ready to join edges 7 and 8. Pinch these together and whipstitch them closed. Take a few extra stitches at the end to secure—knot the thread if you want to, but do not cut it yet.

4. Push the 1⅜" square of template plastic into the bottom of the cube. The plastic will be held in place by the stuffing and helps the cube to sit flat.

5. If you chose not to punch the top piece, cut a 2" square from your leftover weavers cloth or a fabric that coordinates with your pattern colors for the top of the cube. Fold under a ¼" seam allowance so that the square measures the same as the bottom and sides of the cube. Press firmly to give yourself a nice sharp crease for sewing.

6. Beginning where you previously left off, whipstitch the top of the cube in place, stitching along three sides only. If the top piece is attached already (as in a six-sided piece), stitch only two sides. Take a few extra stitches in each corner for security.

7. With the last top edge open, stuff the cube using small amounts of fiberfill at a time. The opening is small and you may have to squeeze the cube slightly to make the opening larger. Use a cuticle stick to push the stuffing into the corners.

Stuff, Stuff, Stuff!

The cube is small, but it may seem like a bottomless pit! To work well as a pincushion, it needs to feel firm, not mushy, when you squeeze the sides.

8. When the cube is filled almost to overflowing, sew the last edge closed. Sweep stray bits of fiberfill in with your needle as you go. Knot and bury your thread inside, and your pincushion is ready to use!

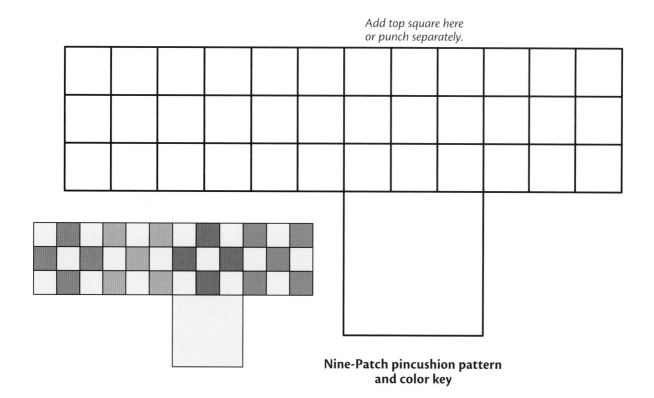

**Nine-Patch pincushion pattern
and color key**

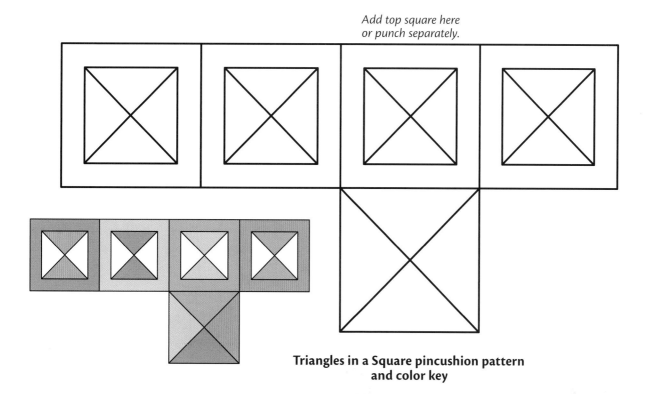

**Triangles in a Square pincushion pattern
and color key**

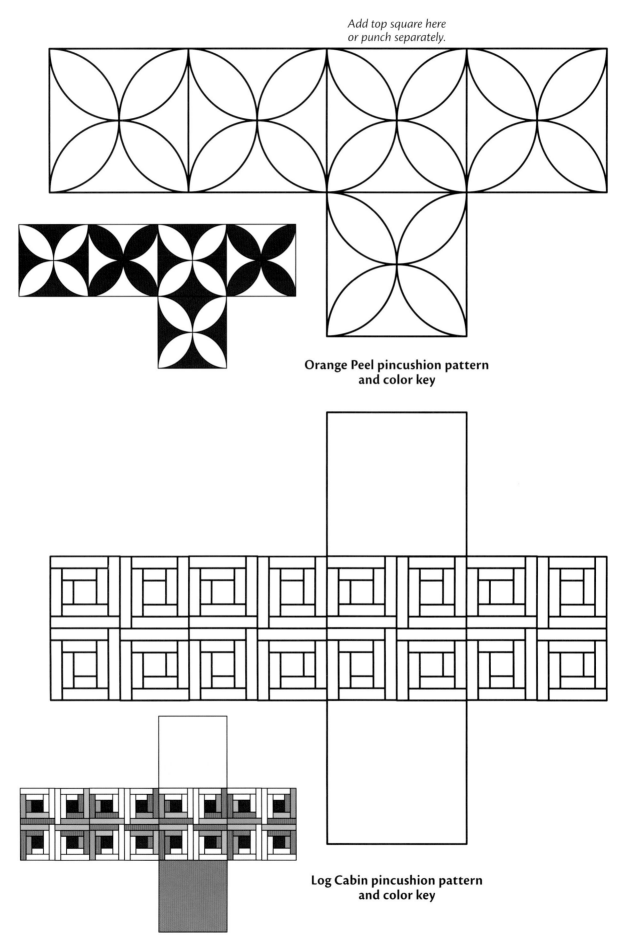

*Add top square here
or punch separately.*

**Orange Peel pincushion pattern
and color key**

**Log Cabin pincushion pattern
and color key**

Round Pincushion

Even Easier

Set of round pincushions • Finished size of punching: approximately 6" x 1½"

I got distracted one day and accidentally cut too much off the paper pattern for a cube pincushion. The long rectangular shape lay curled up on the floor, and I realized that it could be the base of a round pincushion. A little measuring for the top and bottom circles, and voilà! If you choose to make a freehand design such as the color wave or the mountains, bring the ends of the rectangle together and make sure the pattern lines match up along the edges. That way when the sides are sewn together, it will be impossible to tell where the seam is. The pattern can be designed as quilt squares with movement, like the flying geese. Just as with the cube pincushion, you can punch the top, the bottom, or both, but be sure to decide which will be the bottom and sew it on first. Other options include making this into an ornament—perhaps a drum design with a folded ribbon sewn into the seam of the top circle? Have fun coming up with your own ideas.

Materials

- 8" embroidery hoop
- 10" square of weavers cloth or other fabric for each pincushion
- Marking pen or pencil
- Punchneedle with medium (3-strand) needle
- Fabric glue
- Cuticle stick
- 2" square of template plastic for each pincushion
- Sewing needle and thread
- Fiberfill

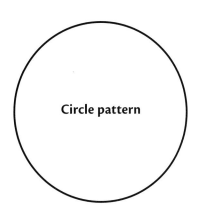

Circle pattern

Pincushion	DMC	Anchor	Weeks	2-ply Yarn
EMBROIDERY FLOSS (3 Strands) or YARN (1 Strand)				
This chart lists floss and yarn selections from various suppliers. For each pincushion, choose one supplier. The box where the supplier column and pincushion row intersect shows the colors you'll need.				
Flying Geese	3752, 801	144, 358		Blue, brown
Color Wave	3078, 727, 725, 741, 776, 3853, 353		6650-Buttercup, 1115-Banana Pops, 2223-Saffron, 2226-Carrot, 2234-Autumn Leaves, 6850-Bluecoat Red, 2278-Hibiscus	
Purple Mountains			1317-Eggplant, 1311-Taffeta, 1318-Concord, 2321-Plum, 1156-Grape Ice, 2334-Lilac, 4125-Snowflake, 1086-Icicle, 2109-Morris Blue	

Punching the Design

1. Trace the pattern onto the weavers cloth, centering the design in the fabric square. Try to position the straight edge of the pattern so it follows a thread. The top and bottom circles can be transferred to the fabric as well, even if you do not plan to punch them. Leave ½" between each pattern. Place the fabric in the hoop with the design in the center. See "Using the Hoop" on page 10.

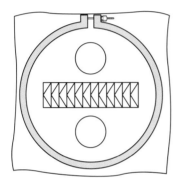

2. Start with one color, punch an outline row, and then fill each section for that color. Continue until all sections are punched.

3. After the design is completely punched, follow the instructions in "Almost Finished" on page 14.

4. Cut out the punched work, leaving a generous ¼" seam allowance around all edges. Carefully fold each side to the back along the edge of the loops and press. Use the cuticle stick to hold the edge down as you press. Pressing gives a sharp crease, which makes a nice sewing line to follow.

5. Even if you did not punch your circle, it needs to be cut out with a ¼" seam allowance. Cut notches into the seam allowance so that it can be folded in without too many lumps. Press for a sharp crease.

Constructing the Pincushion

1. Starting at one end of the rectangle, whipstitch the rectangle to the bottom circle. Use your needle to sweep any stray loops out of the way. As you reach the other end of the rectangle, take a few extra stitches to secure. Sew the side seam. Knot and leave the thread tail hanging inside.

Sewing Circles

Circles have a funny way of getting smaller as you sew around them. Every few stitches, wrap the remaining edge of the rectangle around the remaining edge of the circle to make sure one edge is not getting smaller or larger. If it is, take smaller stitches in the shorter side and slightly larger stitches in the other until they are even again.

2. Cut out a circle from the template plastic to place in the bottom of the pincushion. It should be slightly smaller than the bottom.

3. Whipstitch the top circle until you're halfway around. Take an extra stitch to secure. Squeeze the sides together slightly to enlarge the opening, and stuff the shape with fiberfill. Use your cuticle stick to help fill it firmly.

4. When the cube is filled almost to overflowing, sew the remainder of the circle closed. Use your needle to sweep stray bits of fiberfill inside as you go. Knot and bury your thread inside. Stick your needle into your new pincushion!

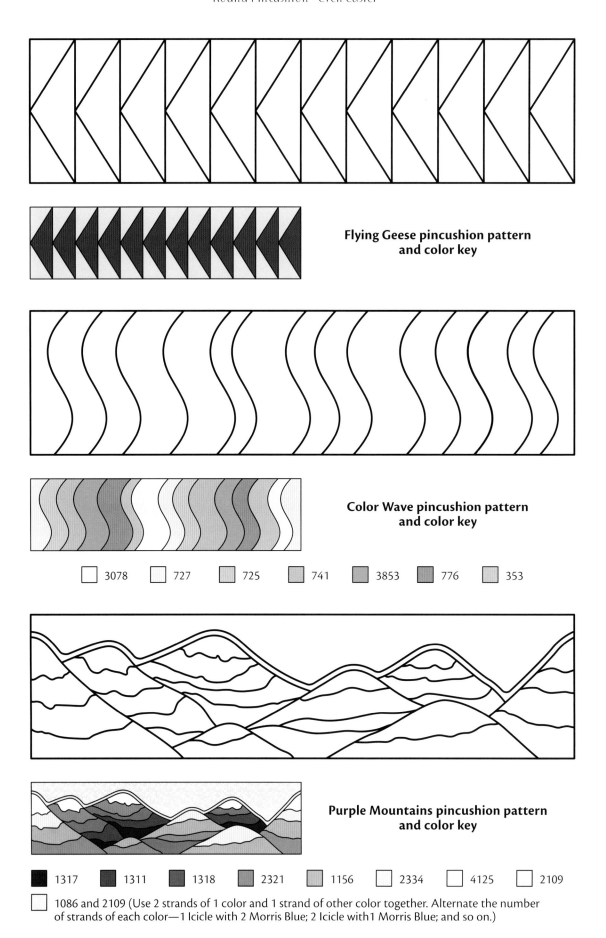

**Flying Geese pincushion pattern
and color key**

**Color Wave pincushion pattern
and color key**

☐ 3078 ☐ 727 ☐ 725 ☐ 741 ☐ 3853 ☐ 776 ☐ 353

**Purple Mountains pincushion pattern
and color key**

☐ 1317 ☐ 1311 ☐ 1318 ☐ 2321 ☐ 1156 ☐ 2334 ☐ 4125 ☐ 2109

☐ 1086 and 2109 (Use 2 strands of 1 color and 1 strand of other color together. Alternate the number of strands of each color—1 Icicle with 2 Morris Blue; 2 Icicle with 1 Morris Blue; and so on.)

Strawberry and Scissors Case

Yummy

Tucked away in a handmade case, your scissors are always right at hand.
The punched strawberry pincushion is a cute decoration.
Finished size of strawberry: approximately 1¾" tall

Who doesn't love strawberries? That sweet, tart flavor goes with almost everything. Even in the middle of winter, it's a real pick-me-up! Make your own strawberry as a cheerful reminder of summer the whole year through. Since the top of the strawberry is left unpunched, choose a leafy green fabric to make the strawberry. Make a few trial punches to test the fabric first. If it will not hold the loops, iron lightweight interfacing to the wrong side and mark your pattern on the interfacing.

With no machine quilting or buttonhole making required for the scissors case, it is especially quick and easy! After turning it inside out, you don't even have to sew the open edge closed. A coordinating button is all you need to sew your case together in one corner. Attach the scissors case and the strawberry to opposite ends of a narrow ribbon. Loop the ribbon around your neck to keep your scissors, pins, and needles handy for all your sewing projects.

Materials

For the strawberry:
- 6" embroidery hoop
- 8" square of green fabric (makes 2)
- Marking pen or pencil
- Punchneedle with medium (3-strand) needle
- Fabric glue
- Fiberfill
- Cuticle stick
- Sewing needle and thread
- Ribbon and large-eye needle

For the scissors case:
- 2 pieces of fabric and stiff interfacing, each 6" x 7"
- Needle and thread
- Straight pin
- Button, ¼" diameter

EMBROIDERY FLOSS (3 Strands) or YARN (1 Strand)			
This chart lists floss selections from various suppliers. For each strawberry, choose one supplier. The box where the supplier column and strawberry row intersect shows the colors you'll need.			
Pincushion	**DMC**	**Anchor**	**Weeks**
Strawberry	816, 310	44, 236	2265-Strawberry Fields, 1298-Gunmetal

Punching the Design

1. Transfer the pattern and cutting line onto your fabric. The pattern is small enough that two will fit in the hoop circle. The bottom edges of each strawberry should be about 1" apart. Place the fabric in the hoop with the design in the center. See "Using the Hoop" on page 10.

2. If you want the strawberry to have seeds, punch those first with black, and then fill in with red.

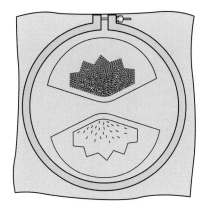

3. After each design is completely punched, follow the instructions in "Almost Finished" on page 14.

4. Carefully cut along the cutting line. Do not follow the outer angles as a cutting line; you will cut off part of the top! Clip, fold, and press the bottom and sides of the design to the back. Trim the excess fabric ¾" from the tip of the points.

5. Pinch the strawberry together with the loops on the outside, and match up the top edges of the punched design. Whipstitch from the bottom to ¾" from the top of the punched edge. Knot the thread at the top and leave the tail on the inside.

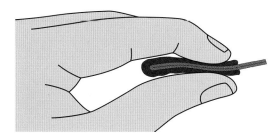

6. Fold the top edge in ¼". With the large-eye needle threaded with ribbon and the end unknotted, sew a large (almost ¼" apart) running stitch around the top edge. Leave both ribbon ends hanging.

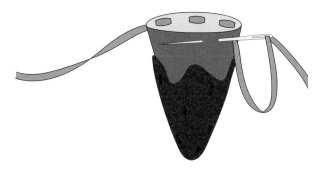

7. Stuff with fiberfill until the strawberry is firm and almost overflowing, using your cuticle stick to help you. Pull one end of the ribbon so that there is about 6" remaining on the other end, then draw the ribbon ends tight, tucking any escaping fiberfill back into the strawberry.

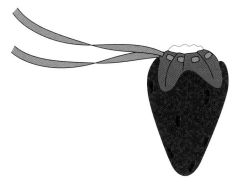

8. Tie both ends into a knot. If desired, tie the ends into a double bow and trim the short end. The long ribbon end will be used to attach the strawberry to the scissors case.

Constructing the Scissors Case

1. Choose one 6" x 7" piece of fabric for the outside of the case and use the other fabric for the inside. On the wrong side of one fabric, trace the pattern, marking the start and end points as indicated on the pattern. Place the fabrics right sides together on top of the interfacing. Use a straight pin to hold the layers in place. Cut along the traced line.

2. Beginning at the start point, sew with a ¼" seam allowance in the direction indicated on the pattern. Stop at the end point. Backstitch at the start and end points. Turn the fabrics inside out, use your cuticle stick to push out the points, and press.

3. Fold in the side with the open edge first, and then fold the other side on top as shown. Pinch the bottom to make the folds smooth at the point.

4. With needle and thread, sew a button in the upper corner. Place your fingers inside the case to make sure you sew through both of the folded sides, but not through the back of the case. Knot and bury the thread.

5. Using the large-eye needle, sew the ribbon through the top of the back of the case. One end should be much longer than the other. Knot and tie in a double bow if desired. Trim the short end and leave the long end hanging.

6. Hold the long ribbon ends from the case and the strawberry together around your neck. Measure the desired length that each should hang on either side of your neck. Tie in a knot and trim the excess ribbon.

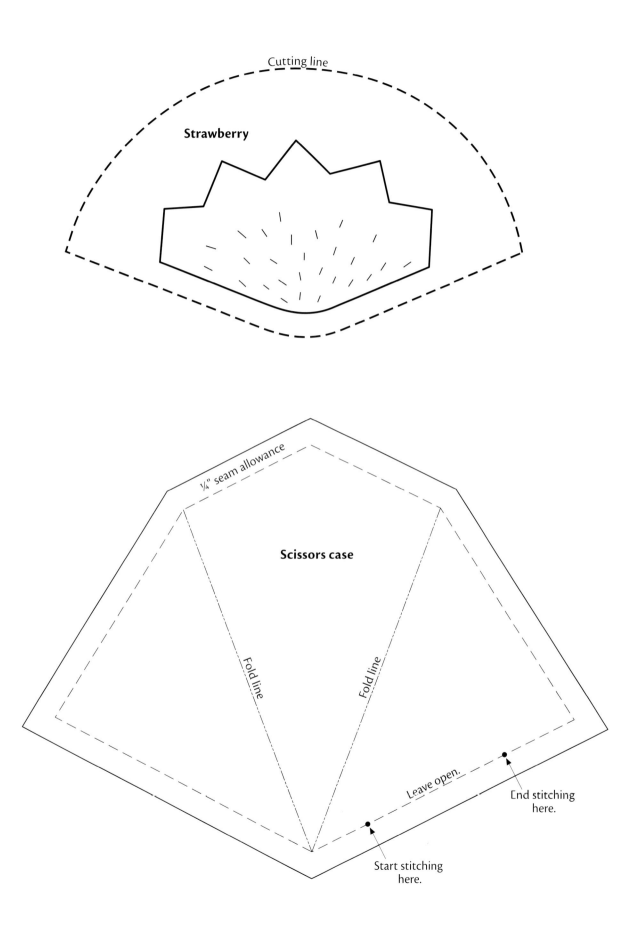

Cutting line

Strawberry

¼" seam allowance

Scissors case

Fold line

Fold line

Leave open.

Start stitching here.

End stitching here.

Resources

www.aleenes.com

Aleene's makes a glue product for nearly every purpose. You can find them in most craft stores.

www.dmc.com

DMC embroidery floss is carried in many craft, needlework, and discount stores. There are hundreds of solid, variegated, and sparkling six-strand floss colors, as well as pearl cottons.

www.coatsandclark.com

Among the well-known products from Coats and Clarks is not only Anchor six-strand embroidery floss in hundreds of solid and variegated colors, but also Susan Bates Hoop-La embroidery hoops. These are available in many craft, needlework, and discount stores.

www.clover-usa.com

The Mesh Transfer Canvas and the Bags & Totes Magnet Tote Bag Closure, along with many other Clover notions, can be found in most craft and needlework stores.

www.gingher.com

Look for Gingher's quality scissors and thread clips in craft, quilt, and needlework shops.

www.junetailor.com

Fray Block and many other June Tailor sewing products are sold in most craft stores.

www.prymdritz.com

Liquid Stitch

This product, which repairs rips in fabric, is found in most discount and craft stores.

www.punchneedlemarketplace.com

Brohman's Inc.
333-335 Pam Dr.
Derrien Springs, MI 49103

The Punch Needle Marketplace is *the* place to go for nearly every punchneedle brand available today, as well as tons of two-ply acrylic yarns. They carry anything and everything to do with punchneedle embroidery and are an incredibly friendly source of massive amounts of information as well as products.

www.weeksdyeworks.com

Weeks Dye Works Inc.
1510-103 Mechanical Blvd.
Garner, NC 27529

For hundreds of beautiful hand-dyed six-strand embroidery flosses and pearl cottons, as well as more than a dozen hand-dyed colors of weavers cloth, look no further than Weeks. If you can't find these in your local quilt shop, contact Weeks directly for a catalog.

About the Author

AMY BELL BUEHLER grew up in North Carolina, with a move to the mountains of Virginia while still a teenager. She and her husband married after they both graduated from Guilford College in Greensboro, North Carolina, and settled in New Jersey. When her boys were toddlers, Amy discovered quilting and all other hobbies fell by the wayside. As a stay-at-home mother, she spent her free time learning new techniques and finding new places to hide her growing stash of fabric. Traditional patterns and reproductions of antique quilts were her focus for many years.

Several years ago her daughter, Mae, was diagnosed with retinitis pigmentosa, a progressive degeneration of the retina resulting in gradual vision loss, and Amy began using modern fabrics with bright colors and patterns in her quilts. "Mae's Cats," featuring whimsical appliquéd cats based on drawings made by Mae, won a blue ribbon in the 2005 New Jersey State

Guild Quilt Show and was juried into the 2006 AQS Show in Paducah, Kentucky. It was also featured in the August 2006 issue of *Quilter's Home* magazine. Amy has recently designed several quilts for Pickle Road Studios.

Although Amy picked up a punchneedle on a whim, her interest in it quickly grew and now nearly every table surface in her home overflows with threads, yarns, and sketches. Two or three hoops hold projects in progress. The family has gotten used to the gentle sound of punching every evening. Besides quilting and punchneedle, Amy also buys and sells Singer featherweight sewing machines when the opportunity strikes. She occasionally teaches a class at her local quilt shop on maintaining these machines.

You can contact Amy at abbuehler@hotmail.com with questions or comments.